PANDAS AT RISK

Clare Hibbert

PowerKiDS press

New York

Published in 2015 by

The Rosen Publishing Group, Inc.

29 East 21st Street, New York, NY 10010

Library of Congress Cataloging-in-Publication Data

Hibbert, Clare, 1970- author.
  Pandas at risk / Clare Hibbert.
      pages cm. — (Save the animals)
  Includes bibliographical references and index.
ISBN 978-1-4777-5913-4 (pbk.)
ISBN 978-1-4777-5909-7 (6 pack)
ISBN 978-1-4777-5911-0 (library binding)
1. Giant panda—Infancy—China—Wolong Shi—
Juvenile literature. 2. Giant panda—Breeding—
Juvenile literature. 3. Giant panda—Conservation—
China—Wolong Shi—Juvenile literature. 4. Wildlife
conservation—China—Wolong Shi—Juvenile
literature. I. Title.
  QL737.C27H53 2015
  599.789—dc23
                                        2014026397

Copyright © 2015 by
The Rosen Publishing Group, Inc.

First published in 2015 by Franklin Watts
Copyright © Arcturus Holdings Limited

Editor: Joe Harris
Picture researcher: Clare Hibbert
Designer: Tokiko Morishima

Picture credits: all images Eric Baccega/Nature PL
except pages 2–3: Pete Oxford/Nature PL and pages
5 (bg) and 14-15 (bg): Shutterstock. Cover image:
Pete Oxford/Nature PL

Manufactured in the United States of America

CPSIA Compliance Information: Batch #CW15PK: For Further Information contact
Rosen Publishing, New York, New York at 1-800-237-9932

CONTENTS

PANDA CENTERS

The forests of South Central China are home to one of the world's favorite animals, the giant panda. Pandas are beautiful, black-and-white bears that are endangered in the wild. Many people are working to help save them.

The giant panda is China's national animal. When the Chinese government saw the danger the panda was in, it created protected areas of forest called reserves. These areas are home to a small number of panda centers. At the centers, experts look after pandas in captivity. They study the pandas and help them to have babies. This work helps to stop panda numbers falling even lower.

For a long time, China's most famous panda center was the Wolong Panda Reserve in Sichuan Province. Sadly, a huge earthquake hit the region in 2008 and damaged the center so badly it had to close down. Luckily, there was already a new center nearby, Bifengxia Panda Center. Chengdu Panda Base is another center in Sichuan Province that is carrying on the work.

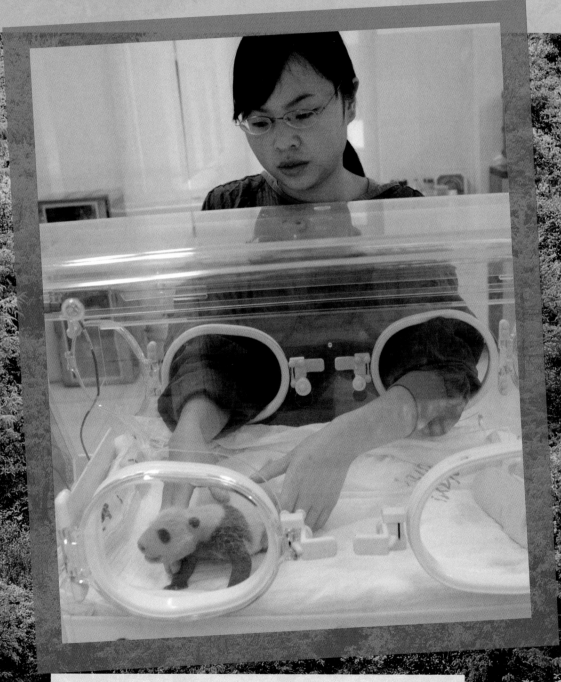

A keeper nurses a baby panda at Bifengxia Giant Panda Breeding and Conservation Center.

THREATS TO PANDAS

The biggest threat to giant pandas is the loss of their habitat. Bamboo forests once covered much of central China. Today, just a few pockets remain, high in the mountains. They are home to the last 1,600 wild pandas.

There are many reasons why the bamboo forests have been chopped down. Bamboo is a useful fuel and building material. However, the main reason for the deforestation was to make way for new roads, villages, farms and cities. Areas where pandas once roamed free now have many busy industries.

The pandas in the last areas of forest are stranded. They cannot move to new feeding grounds. More importantly, they can only choose a mate from the small group of pandas in their own patch. The lack of choice of mates may lead to health problems in their offspring (children).

Fact File: Panda Reserves

In 1963, the Chinese government set up the first panda reserve in Wolong Nature Reserve. It covers 495,000 acres (200,000 hectares) and is home to more than 4,000 species — not just pandas but also golden cats, red pandas, and golden snub-nosed monkeys. Since then, about 40 more bamboo forest reserves have been set up.

A DIET OF BAMBOO

Another problem that faces giant pandas is that they are very picky eaters. Pandas are part of the bear family, so their teeth are designed for meat-eating. They very rarely eat meat, though — **99** percent of their diet is bamboo.

Pandas feed on bamboo leaves, stems, and shoots. Bamboo is not very nourishing, so an adult panda has to eat 26–84 pounds (12–38 kg) a day. Pandas have special "thumbs" on their front paws, which other bears don't have, that help them to grip the bamboo. They also have very powerful jaw muscles and large molars (crushing teeth) to help them break down the tough leaves and stems.

Every 20 years or so, all the bamboo plants of a particular species flower at once, scatter their seeds and then die. In the past, pandas simply moved on to new areas of forest and ate new kinds of bamboo while the old species grew back. In recent times, this has not always been possible because the areas of forest are not connected anymore.

BREEDING PANDAS

The researchers at the panda centers run important breeding programs. For many years it was almost impossible to breed giant pandas in captivity, but recently centers have been having more success.

Some mammals can become pregnant at any time of the year and produce lots of babies each time. Rabbits and mice are good examples. Pandas are not like that. A female panda can only mate successfully for two or three days each year. Researchers can run tests to learn when is the best time for her to mate.

A keeper feeds pandas at the Chengdu Research Base of Giant Panda Breeding.

Pandas are used to being on their own. A male and female may need a lot of encouragement to mate during the short time that the female's body is ready. If all goes well, four or five months later the female will give birth to one or two cubs.

Fact File: Communication
In the wild, pandas find a mate by scent and by sound — they bleat and chirp. Pandas use calls to communicate at other times too. They produce more than ten different sounds for different situations.

NEWBORN PANDAS

Newborn panda cubs are small enough to stretch out on an adult human's hand. They are completely helpless and rely on their mother for food, warmth, and protection. They are born with their eyes tightly shut and they cry a lot.

Panda mothers can give birth to one or two cubs. Each is just 6 inches (15 cm) long. Sadly, if twins are born in the wild, only one cub survives. The mother cannot produce enough milk to feed both babies, because her diet of bamboo is not nourishing enough. Instead, the new mom concentrates on caring for the stronger of the two cubs.

In the panda centers, however, twins can survive. The mother cares for one cub while the caretakers raise the other one in an incubator – a special cot used for medical care. After a week, the caretakers swap the two cubs. The first goes into the incubator, and the second spends time with its mom. A week later, they switch back again. This means that both cubs receive milk from their mother and bond with her.

FEEDING TIME

Pandas are mammals, so the cubs feed on mother's milk. Like all babies, they are growing fast but they have small tummies — that means they need to eat small amounts very often.

Newborn panda cubs feed six to 14 times a day, sometimes suckling for as long as half an hour at a time. That does not leave the mother much chance to feed herself in the first few weeks! She never leaves her baby for longer than a couple of hours. By the age of two months, the cub feeds only three to four times a day.

At the panda centers, cubs are fed by their mothers or with special powdered milk formula. The formula was developed by experts at the San Diego Zoo in the United States. It is a close copy of real panda milk and very rich in fats.

Fact File: Panda Diet

Milk is the cubs' main food for the first year, but from six months they eat some bamboo too. Weaning (giving up milk) happens between 18 months and two years. In captivity, pandas eat other foods besides bamboo, including eggs, minced meat, and bread with added vitamins.

GROWING STRONGER

For the first couple of months, cubs stay in an incubator or with their mother in her enclosure (a walled area). They are looked after round the clock, either by their mom or their human caretakers. Slowly, they grow stronger.

Newborn panda cubs look pink because they only have a very fine, thin covering of white hair over their pink skin. When they are about a week old, the cubs start to grow black fur around their eyes, on their ears, and around their shoulders. Over the next couple of weeks, the areas of black thicken and spread, until the panda's legs and chest are covered too.

For at least the first month, the panda cubs are blind. Their eyes half-open at 30 to 45 days old, then open fully a week or two later. For the first couple of months, the cubs just eat and sleep. They are very weak. By 75 to 80 days the cubs start to take their first steps. Their teeth begin to come through and their eyesight and hearing improve.

A six-week old panda in an incubator at Bifengxia Panda Center.

BETTER CARE

Breeding centers are now amazingly successful at raising cubs in captivity. This is good news for these endangered bears. Only a couple of decades ago, it was a very different story.

In the past, few cubs survived beyond five months. Centers now have a success rate of around 90 percent. One reason is that the cubs' formula milk is better suited to their needs. Before, babies were fed formula based on cows' or dogs' milk.

Another problem in the past was that caretakers were feeding babies that were still full from their last meal. They had not noticed that panda mothers lick their babies to encourage them to empty their bowels. Now caretakers rub the cubs' tummies to make them go to the bathroom before feeding.

READY TO EXPLORE

By the age of four to five months, the panda babies are much more active. They are moving around a lot now. In the wild, they would be trotting behind their mother in the forest and climbing trees.

The staff move the babies into the nursery. Here, the babies can practice crawling, walking and sitting up. They are very clumsy at first! The staff split the play space with see-through screens. This means each panda has its own safe space, but it can see the others and get used to being around them. It also means the cubs cannot hurt each other, either accidentally or on purpose.

Like most babies, panda cubs love to play. It is how they practice the skills they will need as adults. Playing chase improves their strength and agility. Ball games help them learn to control their paws. Play also helps the cubs become more social – better at being part of a group. This will help when they are moved out to the enclosures.

KEEPERS

Many people work at the panda centers. Some are paid staff members and others are volunteers. Together, they have many different skills. The thing they all have in common is a passion for pandas.

Bifengxia Panda Center has around 150 staff members. They look after the adults in the breeding center, the newborns in the incubator rooms, and the larger cubs in the nurseries. There are also larger pandas to care for, which live in indoor and outdoor enclosures.

Bifengxia needs to have some staff there 24 hours a day, seven days a week. As well as feeding all the animals and keeping their incubators or enclosures clean, there is work looking after sick or injured pandas in the panda hospital. Bifengxia has a research center too, where scientists are studying pandas.

Fact File: Bifengxia

Building work began on Bifengxia Panda Center in 2002 because the Wolong center was full. Scientists split Wolong's panda population between the two centers. When the 2008 earthquake struck, some Wolong staff and pandas lost their lives. All the remaining pandas were moved to Bifengxia.

PLAYING OUTSIDE

By the age of one, the cubs weigh around 75 pounds (34 kg) and have stopped feeding on milk. In the wild, they would still be with their mother at this age. At the panda centers, the youngsters are moved into large enclosures that have outside space.

From the age of one to about five, the pandas are known as juveniles (youngsters) and then sub-adults. They can look after themselves but they are not yet adults. They are still growing. As adults, they will weigh 175–330 pounds (80–150 kg). Juveniles and sub-adults like to play. They chase each other and tumble on the ground. They like to gnaw on sturdy chew toys too.

The young pandas would not be living so close to other pandas if they were in the wild. But their enclosures are designed to be as similar to their wild habitat as possible. Hopefully, the pandas will keep their natural instincts. They can feed themselves from the bamboo plants in their enclosure and they can try out their climbing skills on the climbing frames.

PANDA SOCIETY

In the wild, adult pandas live on their own. They only come together to mate. Mothers and cubs separate not long after the cubs are weaned, somewhere between the ages of 18 months and three years.

In captivity, life is different because the pandas live in shared enclosures. However, they do the same things they would do in the wild. Older pandas spend most of the day resting, looking for food or eating. Youngsters use their time to work out their place in panda society!

Two juvenile pandas play-fighting

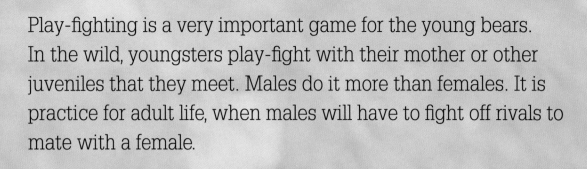

Play-fighting is a very important game for the young bears. In the wild, youngsters play-fight with their mother or other juveniles that they meet. Males do it more than females. It is practice for adult life, when males will have to fight off rivals to mate with a female.

Fact File: Panda Territory
In the wild, each adult panda has its own territory. They mark the edges to warn other pandas to keep out. They spray scent from their scent glands and make scratch marks on tree trunks with their claws. A male panda's territory might overlap the territories of several females.

27

SPREADING THE WORD

Pandas are an important symbol of conservation. The World Wide Fund for Nature (WWF) has used a picture of a panda on its logo since it began in 1961. People all over the world are fascinated by pandas and would love to see one close up.

Panda centers enable tourists to see pandas for themselves. Visitors can observe the pandas in an environment that is as close as possible to their natural habitat. Panda centers are able to make a lot of money by letting in tourists. This helps towards the costs of looking after the pandas. It goes towards the panda center's conservation work, breeding programs, and research.

Pandas face an uncertain future, with just 1,600 left in the wild. The panda centers are doing important work by breeding pandas in captivity. Scientists are able to study these captive pandas. They will soon have measured the complete DNA code for pandas. This information can help them find new ways to save pandas. It will be especially important if pandas become extinct in the wild.

GLOSSARY

AGILITY The ability to move quickly and easily.

BREEDING PROGRAM A plan to produce baby animals, for example endangered animals.

CONSERVATION Protecting and keeping something for the future.

DEFORESTATION Chopping down an area's natural forests.

DNA The substance found in the control center (nucleus) of a living cell that carries the instructions needed to build and run a living thing.

ENCLOSURE An area with a wall or fence around it.

EXTINCT Having disappeared forever.

HABITAT The place where an animal or plant lives.

INCUBATOR A tank-like cot for newborns that keeps them warm and supplied with oxygen.

JUVENILE In pandas, a youngster between the ages of one year and 18 months.

LOGO A symbol that represents an organization.

MOLAR One of the wide chewing teeth at the back of the jaw.

PLAY-FIGHTING Pretend fighting, where the animals can practice without causing any injuries.

RESERVE An area where the land and its wildlife are being saved for the future, by the government or another organization.

RIVAL An animal that is competing with another animal for the same thing.

SCENT GLAND Part of an animal that produces a smelly substance.

SPECIES A group of similar organisms that can reproduce together.

SUB-ADULT In pandas, a youngster between the ages of 18 months and about five years.

TERRITORY The area over which an animal travels in its searches for food and a mate.

VOLUNTEER Someone who works for free. Volunteers at panda centers often pay to stay there and work, and that money goes towards running the centers.

WEANING Stopping a baby from feeding on mother's milk and introducing it to solid foods.

FURTHER INFORMATION

FURTHER READING

A Visual Celebration of Giant Pandas by Fanny Lai and Bjorn Olesen
(Editions Didier Millet Pty, 2013)

Endangered Pandas by John Crossingham and Bobbie Kalman (Crabtree, 2005)

Giant Pandas by Heather Angel (Evans Mitchell Books, 2005)

Mammals of China by Andrew T Smith (Princeton University Press, 2013)

National Geographic Readers: Pandas by Anne Schreiber
(National Geographic Society, 2010)

Panda Rescue by Dan Bortolotti (Firefly Books, 2004)

WEBSITES

Due to the changing nature of Internet links, PowerKids Press has developed an online list of websites related to the subject of this book. This site is updated regularly. Please use this link to access the list:

www.powerkidslinks.com/sta/panda

INDEX